Congratulations
Bruce
you are a Grenadier Survivor.
Our City will also survive.

2011

[signature]

CHRISTCHURCH

Beyond the **Cordon**

222

CHRISTCHURCH

Beyond the Cordon

22.2

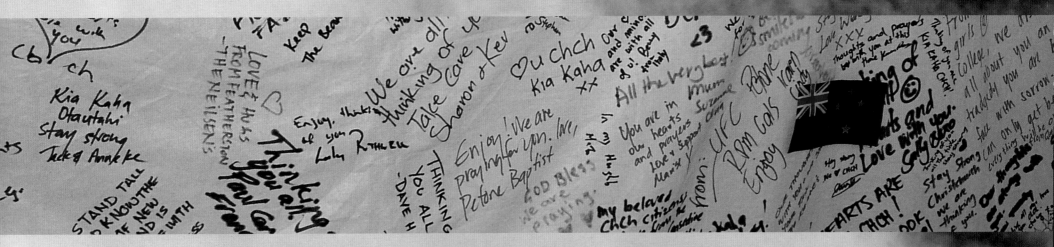

THROUGH THE EYES OF THE NEW ZEALAND POLICE PHOTOGRAPHERS

Hodder Moa

National Library of New Zealand Cataloguing-in-Publication Data

Christchurch 22.2 : beyond the cordon / New Zealand Police.

ISBN 978-1-86971-255-6

1. Christchurch Earthquake, N.Z., 2011—Pictorial works. 2. Search
and rescue operations—New Zealand—Christchurch—Pictorial works.
3. Earthquake damage—New Zealand—Christchurch—Pictorial works.
4. Christchurch (N.Z.)—Pictorial works.
I. New Zealand Police.

993.8304—dc 22

A Hodder Moa Book

Published in 2011 by Hachette New Zealand Ltd

4 Whetu Place, Mairangi Bay

Auckland, New Zealand

www.hachette.co.nz

Introduction written by Peter Burdon

Designed and produced by Book Design Ltd, Christchurch, www.bookdesign.co.nz

Printed by Everbest Printing Co. Ltd., China

Front cover: Queensland Urban Search and Rescue teams
   work through the night amidst the smoke and rubble at the
   Canterbury Television (CTV) building site.

Back cover: Police officers look on as wreckage is
   cleared from the Canterbury Television (CTV) site.

This book is dedicated to Sergeant Jerry Rivett, Officer in Charge of the Canterbury Forensic Photography section. Jerry's 34 years with New Zealand Police have included 26 years as a photographer, and he has given inspiring leadership as a tutor, mentor and colleague to Police photographers throughout the country.

Family Help Trust

Royalties from the sale of this publication will go directly to Family Help Trust, which provides early intervention services in Christchurch. Its primary focus is to prevent the maltreatment of children within the city's most vulnerable families.

The Trust's programmes and services are intensive, long-term, family-based and child-focused. They target high-risk parents with multiple-problem histories who have young families, and aim to break the cycles of inter-generational dysfunction.

Family Help Trust is affiliated with Jigsaw, a national umbrella group of child protection services throughout New Zealand.

The Canterbury earthquakes of September 2010 and February 2011 have had an impact on Christchurch families across all walks of life. These events have added significant additional stress to those families that we work with, most of whom have little in the way of personal resources to begin with.

We have been amazed at their remarkable resilience in these challenging times. We are delighted that the royalties will support our continuing work to keep Christchurch children safe.

Libby Robins
Director, Family Help Trust

Breaking the cycle for New Zealand children

Family Help Trust cannot continue to fight the cycle of child abuse, violence, poverty, state-dependency and crime without the financial support of donors.

Your donations and support are welcome. For information on how you can help the Trust please visit the website: www.familyhelptrust.org.nz, or phone +64 3 365 9912.

Foreword

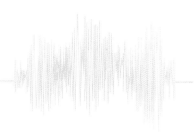

At 12.51pm on 22 February 2011 an earthquake of magnitude 6.3 struck Christchurch, causing widespread damage and the tragic loss of 181 lives.

The event triggered one of the largest emergency response operations ever seen in New Zealand. A national state of emergency was in place for 10 weeks, and thousands of emergency services personnel, engineers, soldiers, contractors and everyday heroes worked around the clock to rescue and recover the lost and missing, make buildings safe, restore essential services and bring relief to the city.

This publication provides a unique window into that operation, and pays tribute to some of the people most closely involved. First is the team of Police Forensic Photographers from Christchurch and around New Zealand ably led by Sergeant Jerry Rivett, a group whose day-to-day work is demanding, often grim, and rarely seen by the public. They worked alongside search and rescue and victim identification teams, documenting the tragic human toll with clarity and compassion.

Secondly, this book acknowledges the work of the Urban Search and Rescue (USAR) and Disaster Victim Identification (DVI) teams. These men and women searched damaged and dangerous buildings, and sifted through tonnes of rubble for days on end, at first looking for survivors and then retrieving the bodies of those who were lost. This was a truly international effort with New Zealand crews joined by USAR teams from Australia,

Singapore, Japan, Taiwan, China, the United States and the United Kingdom, and DVI units from Australia, the United Kingdom, Thailand, Israel, Japan, Korea, China and Singapore.

As District Commander I was immensely proud of the efforts of our local police, supported by colleagues from around New Zealand, who led rescue efforts and provided a reassuring police presence in the city. We were assisted by hundreds of officers from every Australian state and territory, working together for the first time. Our Family Liaison Team also provided invaluable support to the families of those killed in the earthquake.

Gary McCormick's poems make an apt contribution to this book. After the earthquake his poem '22.2.11' seemed to resonate with me, capturing something of the stunned disbelief that we all felt over the devastating events. My thanks to Gary for his support and for these poems.

I'm delighted that royalties from this book will go to Christchurch's Family Help Trust. Police have a long-standing relationship with the Trust, which works directly with local families at risk — and there are so many more of those in the wake of the city's earthquakes. It's heartening that out of tragedy much good can still come.

Superintendent Dave Cliff
Canterbury Police District Commander

Introduction

They worked tirelessly for weeks on end with little sleep in devastating and dangerous conditions. However, the Christchurch Police Forensic Photographers believe they were in a privileged position during the aftermath of the earthquake that ravaged their city on Tuesday, 22 February 2011.

All nine photographers and their colleagues from other parts of New Zealand took pride in their ability to help identify those lost and see them returned to their families. 'We all did the best jobs we could because we knew that might be the difference between someone being identified or lost forever,' said Geoff.

After 10 days working in the makeshift mortuary at Burnham Military Camp, Mike was asked how he coped with this line of work day after day. 'It's about getting bodies home to their loved ones. That's why you do it,' he said.

Although the mortuary was an emotional and intense place in many ways, Phil said it was this identification process that made it worthwhile. 'We were in amongst it, handing back deceased to their families. That's a pretty powerful position to be in,' he said. At the mortuary, John was moved seeing all the bodies and body parts given a blessing from an Army chaplain before the post-mortem procedures began.

Interestingly, not one photograph was taken on the day of the earthquake by the forensic photographers. There were two reasons for this. First, when they evacuated the ninth floor of the Christchurch Central Police Station, their camera equipment was left behind. Secondly, as sworn police officers, the photographers were needed for urgent public safety duties such as moving people away from buildings in the central city.

On that first afternoon, Geoff and Mike had just begun doing crowd control near the Bridge of Remembrance on Cashel Street when a seriously crushed man was brought out of a building on a board. Realising there was no chance of an ambulance arriving, they placed the man on the roof of an unmarked police station-wagon and slowly drove him to Christchurch Hospital. While Mike stayed at the Bridge to help with the crowd, Geoff and members of the public drove down Oxford Terrace, all doors open, doing what they could to comfort the seriously injured man. 'We were going the wrong way down a one-way street, but luckily we managed to weave our way through the traffic,' Geoff said. Two days later Geoff returned to Christchurch Hospital to take some post-mortem pictures, and found one of the bodies was the man he and Mike had tried to save.

The team usually started their day at 8am, but on Wednesday, 23 February, they all arrived before 6am ready to go. Their first problem was getting access to their equipment. The Police building had only been cleared to level three and their gear was on level nine. After they got access, they were each attached to a Disaster Victim Identification (DVI) team, and worked with the teams as they were assigned jobs.

Initially Chris's DVI team spent less time in the field, so he was instrumental in setting up the team's temporary office in the yard behind the Central Police Station. 'It was testament to him that thousands of photographs were able to be used in the identification process,' said head of the Forensic Photography Section, Sergeant Jerry Rivett.

As Forensic Photographers, these men were used to looking at dead bodies, but the volume of work and devastation around them was something new. Phil said after a few days, when the number of bodies to deal with escalated and the state of those bodies coming out of the Canterbury Television (CTV) building became evident, it was harder to deal with. 'At times it felt almost too big to take in. This was our town. It was all so surreal,' he said.

Greg said when he looks through the lens, he is working and manages to keep a professional distance between himself and the victim. 'The difference this time was that when I pulled away from the lens, the devastation was all around me. I couldn't escape from it. Everywhere I looked there was mayhem,' he said.

Phil remembers a conversation with a colleague on the CTV rubble. It was smouldering underneath them with steam escaping, while the building was

still burning. 'I said to Nigel, "I think I know what Hell looks like." He said, "I was just thinking the same thing".'

This highlights the dangers they faced on sites like CTV. On one occasion Mike was hit by a piece of flying concrete. After a body was found, a digger was brought in to remove concrete so the identification process could begin. A piece flew off and hit Mike in the cheekbone. When he tried to walk away, his feet wouldn't move — he had been concussed and required a visit to hospital.

Geoff remembers the dangers of working on the CTV rubble, known as 'the pile'. Apart from splitting his boots from the heat below, there was the constant threat of the damaged structures collapsing — they moved whenever there was an aftershock. An air horn had been set up to signal workers to run if these structures looked like falling. Three blasts meant it was time to go. 'I remember one question was "do we have to wait for the third blast, or can we start running after the first?",' Geoff said.

While the photographers saw themselves as privileged in playing a part in victim identification, they were also the only photographers in the central city 'red zone' for three weeks after the initial earthquake. That meant they were the only ones able to capture events as they unfolded.

'Our work with the DVI teams was our core role, but we were also acutely aware that what was going on around us had to be recorded, otherwise it would never be seen,' Greg said. These images, taken predominantly in the central city where the majority of DVI work was concentrated, are the focus of this book.

Jerry could not have been more proud of his team. He said they were all totally committed to their jobs in difficult circumstances. 'They often worked 14-hour days and put themselves in constant danger, but they never questioned anything they were asked to do. It's also important to remember they are human and had their own families to support throughout the period.' The photographers also acknowledged the tremendous support they had from their own families, which made the demands of the job easier to cope with.

The Christchurch Forensic Photographers and their colleagues from around the country can take deserved credit for their work, contributing to an identification process that saw all but four of the 181 earthquake victims identified.

The Christchurch Forensic Photography team are:

Sergeant Jerry Rivett, Officer in Charge, Forensic Photography, Canterbury
Senior Constable Mike Johnston
Senior Constable Greg Sawtell
Senior Constable John Trenchard
Senior Constable Chris Ellis
Senior Constable Geoff Burns
Constable Phil Little
Constable Guy Wiseman
Constable Charlotte Dyhrberg
Deb Wilson — Photographic Assistant

The additional forensic photographers are:

Senior Constable Bill Allen, Auckland
Senior Constable Don Bruce, Auckland
Constable Briar Douglas, Auckland
Constable Eddie Fields, Dunedin
Senior Constable Nigel Fookes, Hamilton
Senior Constable Chris Gladstone, Nelson
Constable Tracey McCarthy, Auckland
Senior Constable Craig McKersey, Dunedin
Senior Constable Warrick Pearson, Hamilton
Senior Constable Simon Schollum, Timaru
Constable Paula Tanuvasa, Wellington
Senior Constable Nick Voysey, Rotorua
Sergeant Rob Walker, Palmerston North
Sergeant Karl Wilson, Auckland

22.2.11

You miserable, low-life bastard!
We saw you on the fourth of September
crawling into town on your spineless spine.
Giving us a flick, looking us over.

An earthquake straight from the Yellow Pages.
You know the drill:
the torch, the batteries,
the bottles of water.

In September, you were only the piano player,
tinkling the ivories, thin moustache.
Checking us out!
Eyeing the women on the dance floor.

My, oh my, you waited …
Held your venomous tongue in check.
A snake that lived in a crack in the earth.
All black coils and shining musculature.

I saw you whip up a blind alley
Full of hatred and dark breath.
Grim clouds could only pity us.
You held us down on the jagged ground.

Shook the streets and the city buildings.
Ripped the spire from the Cathedral.
All that man had made
was used to batter us.

And all those poor people …
Tourists taking photographs.
Babies taken in pairs.
The hikers in the hills.

The ones buried beneath us still …

You miserable bastard of a thing!

The time has come
said the drummer to the drum,
when I can make no sense of it.

— Gary McCormick

Opposite: Looking south on High Street at the intersection with   and Manchester Streets.

This page: High Street.

Opposite: The Operations Room at Christchurch Central Police Station, at the height of the emergency response.

Top: Police staff muster in the yard at Christchurch Central Police Station.

Bottom: Up-to-date aerial photographs helped the Police Southern Communications Centre despatch units to jobs.

Following pages: Hereford Street, with the Hanafins building (left) and the BNZ (right).

Opposite: Hanafins building, Hereford Street.

This page: City Mall, High Street. Food and drinks were left abandoned at cafes throughout the city. The smell of decaying food was a constant presence for weeks.

Above: City Mall, Cashel Street.
Opposite: City Mall, High Street.

Above: Colombo Street between Lichfield and Tuam Streets.

Opposite: Damaged buses on Colombo Street. Eight people died when masonry fell on to Red Bus number 702.

Opposite and above: Colombo Street.

Above and opposite: Colombo Street, between Tuam and St Asaph Streets.

Whitcoulls building, City Mall, Cashel Street.

City Mall, Cashel Street — a busy shopping precinct where four lives were lost.

Opposite and above: Poplar Lane, between Tuam and Lichfield Streets.

Above and opposite: Police and members of the New Zealand Fire Service USAR team at City Mall, Cashel Street.

Opposite: Manchester Street looking south, the Civic building at centre left.

Above: New Regent Street.

Above and opposite: Colombo Street, between Kilmore and Peterborough Streets.

Chester Street East.

Left: The Clock Tower and Telephone Cabinet, Oxford Terrace.
Right: Interior of St Luke's in the City, corner of Manchester and Kilmore Streets.

Above: Chester Street East.

Opposite: Road damage on Fitzgerald Avenue.

Following pages: Colombo Street, looking north from Gloucester Street.

Opposite: Colombo Street, between Gloucester and Armagh Streets.

Above: Colombo Street, looking south towards the Forsyth Barr building and Cathedral Square.

Above: Colombo Street, looking south from Armagh Street.

Opposite: A Disaster Victim Identification team from the West Coast on Colombo Street, north of Cathedral Square.

Pages 50–69: ChristChurch Cathedral and Cathedral Square.

Above: Floral tributes placed by emergency workers on behalf of victims' families.

CATHEDRAL
VISITORS' CENTRE

Opposite and above: Urban Search and Rescue (USAR) workers stand by as the heavy machinery clears rubble.
The cylindrical structure acts as a protective cage for search teams.

Opposite and above: Cathedral interior.

Top: A Cathedral bell salvaged from the rubble.
Bottom: USAR workers from the United States.

Opposite and above: A steel tunnel provides safe access and shelter for USAR teams inside the Cathedral.

Opposite and above: 'Barney Rubble' — the pigeon rescued from the Cathedral debris, five days after the earthquake.

Opposite and above: The Regent Theatre building (former Royal Exchange) on the western edge of Cathedral Square.

Above: Cathedral Square's much-loved chess set, with the fallen statue of John Robert Godley in the background.

Opposite: Looking east on Worcester Street towards the west wall of ChristChurch Cathedral.

Opposite and above: Our City O-Tautahi, the former
Municipal Chambers, on Worcester Street.

Above and opposite: Smiths City carpark, Dundas Street.

Pages 78–83: The Forsyth Barr building, corner of Armagh and Colombo Streets.

Above and opposite: A United States USAR team inspects collapsed stairwells, inside the Forsyth Barr building.

Above: New Zealand Army personnel and light armoured vehicles (LAVs) assisted on central city cordons.

Opposite: The Cathedral of the Blessed Sacrament, Barbadoes Street.

Pages 86–119: PGC House, the Pyne Gould Corporation building, Cambridge Terrace, where 18 people died.

Opposite and above: Crane operators were a vital part of search efforts, with cranes often providing the only safe access to parts of the site.

Opposite: Looking towards the PGC building across the Avon River, the former Edmonds Band Rotunda (Retour restaurant) at right.

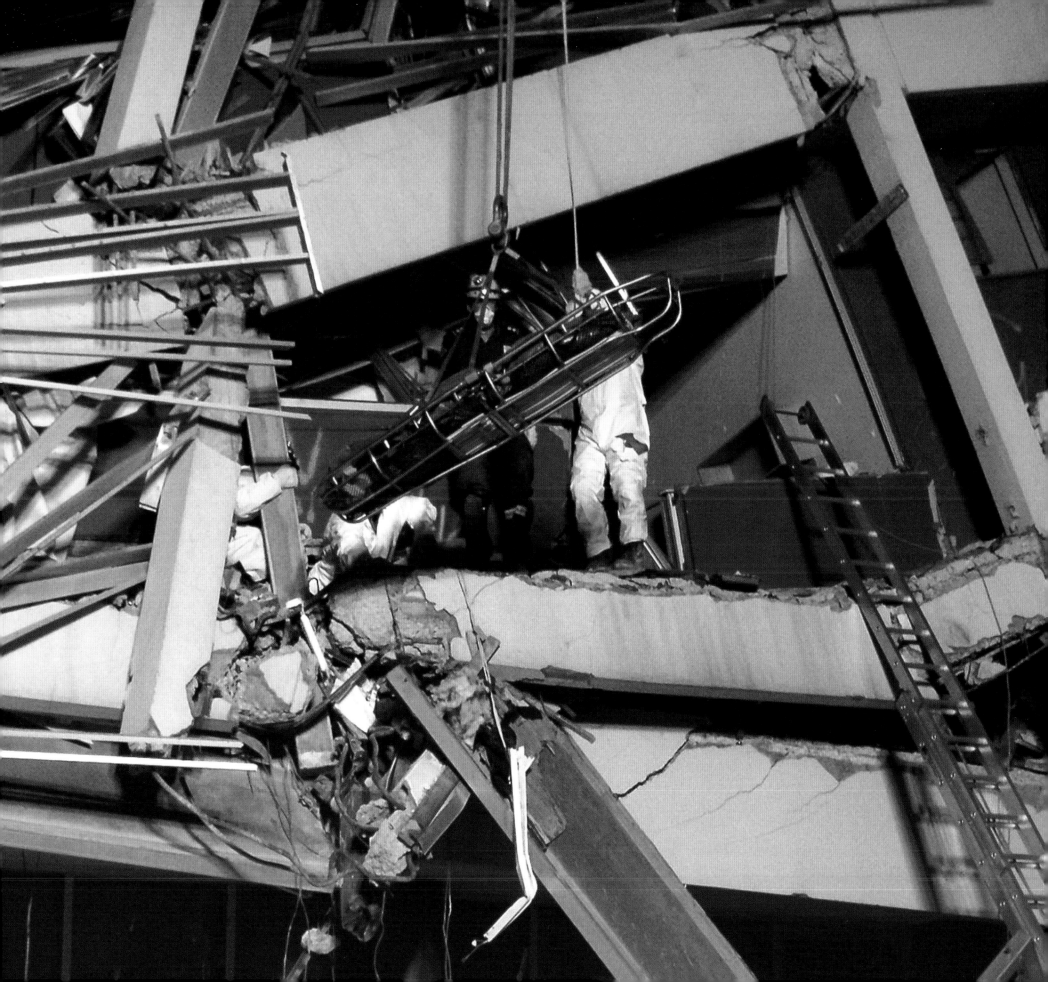

Above and opposite: New Zealand Police DVI teams at work. Photographers documented victims
as well as photographing belongings, personal effects and other items on site.

Above and opposite: New Zealand DVI teams at work and rest.

Opposite and above: Retrieving personal effects was a key step in assisting the victim identification process.

Above: Search dogs, complete with paw protection, were a central part of rescue and recovery efforts.

Opposite and above: The USAR base at Latimer Square.

Above and opposite: The USAR base took on an international flavour with crews from around the world working and relaxing together.

Above and opposite: Tonnes of specialist search equipment arrived with overseas USAR teams, and a sprawling tent city materialised.
Crews brought with them all they needed to remain self-sufficient for weeks.

Above and opposite: St Paul's Trinity Pacific Church, corner of Madras and Cashel Streets.

Pages 128–149: The Canterbury Television (CTV) building, Madras Street, where 115 lives were lost.

Above: A memorial at the CTV site, with tributes and mementos left by victims' families.

Above: The CTV building lift tower stood as an eerie monument over the site for many weeks.

Opposite: The safety siren was a constant reminder of the dangerous conditions crews were working in.

Opposite and above: Thick smoke from the fire which followed the initial earthquake remained a hazard at the CTV site for several days.

Above and opposite: Floodlights were brought in as recovery and DVI efforts continued around the clock, with crews working in three shifts, 24 hours a day.

Opposite and above: Heavy machinery and lifting equipment were essential in helping to clear the CTV site.

Pages 150–161: The USAR team from Japan at work on the CTV site.

Opposite and above: USAR teams worked closely with local contracting firms in the search and recovery operations at the CTV site.

Above right: Markers record the locations of any significant items found during the detailed and time-consuming search.

Opposite: The Japanese USAR team and fellow workers honoured each victim recovered.

Above: An Australian USAR search dog waits to be redeployed on the CTV site.

Opposite: Cycling became a favoured mode of transport for these USAR staff from New South Wales and Queensland.

Opposite and following pages: New Zealand Police DVI teams.

Opposite and above: DVI teams cover every centimetre of the CTV site, removing rubble piece by piece in a painstaking search for evidence.

Above and following pages: The CTV site.

Above: Sparks fly as concrete cutting equipment is pressed into action amidst the tangled wreckage of the CTV building.

Opposite: DVI staff sifting rocks and rubble, ensuring even the smallest items are not overlooked.

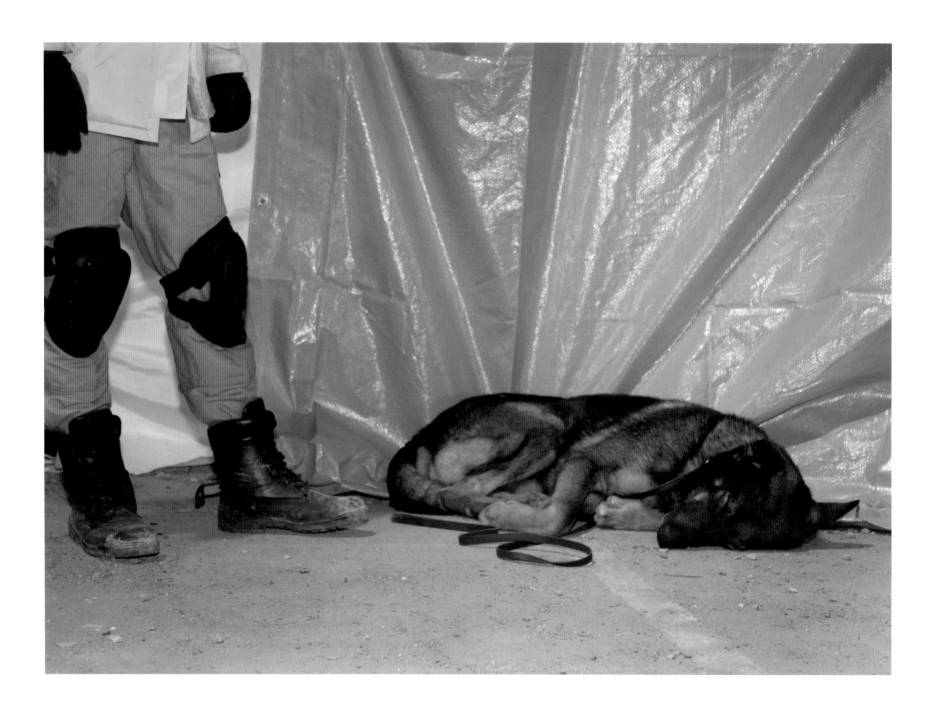

Above: The Queensland USAR team at the CTV site prepares to deploy a probe camera, giving searchers a view into the building debris.

Above and opposite: USAR teams from Japan, China and New Zealand working side by side at the CTV site.

Above and opposite: Japanese USAR team members using concrete cutters at the CTV site.

Opposite and above: With much of the CTV site cleared, USAR teams carry out a detailed grid search.

Above: A Japanese USAR team during the final stages of recovery at the CTV site, using probe cameras to search in the remaining rubble.

Above: Final day at the CTV site — Japanese and Chinese USAR crews say their farewells.

Left: The site is cleared and the final scoop of debris taken away.

Right: New Zealand's DVI team.

Above: An international effort — USAR and DVI teams on the final day at CTV, 5 March 2011.

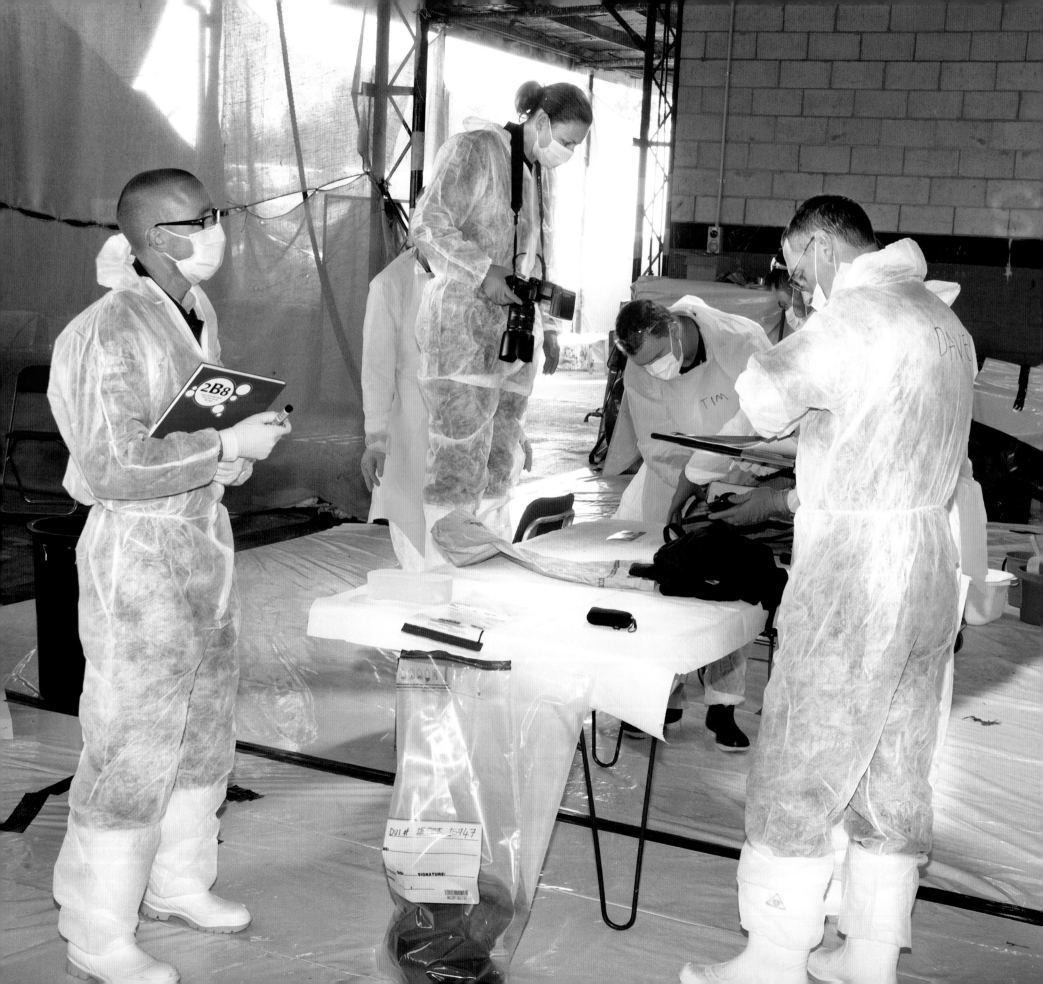

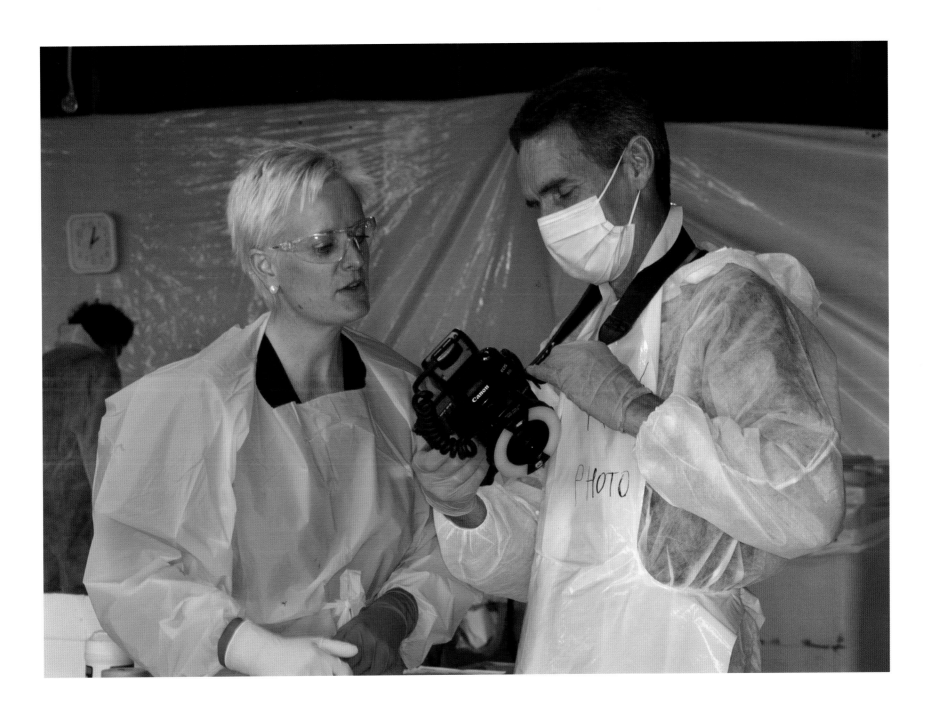

Pages 190–195: The final stage in the victim identification process, at the Burnham Military Camp mortuary facilities.

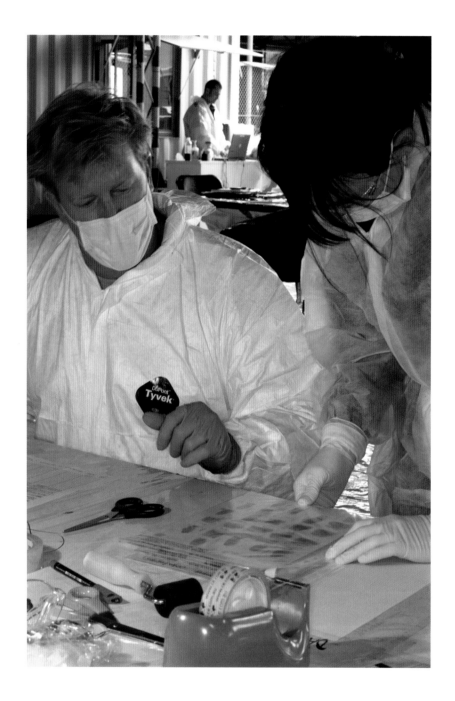

Above and opposite: Forensic specialists analyse fingerprints, DNA, dental records and other information in the effort to reunite families with their lost loved ones. Each step is carefully photographed.

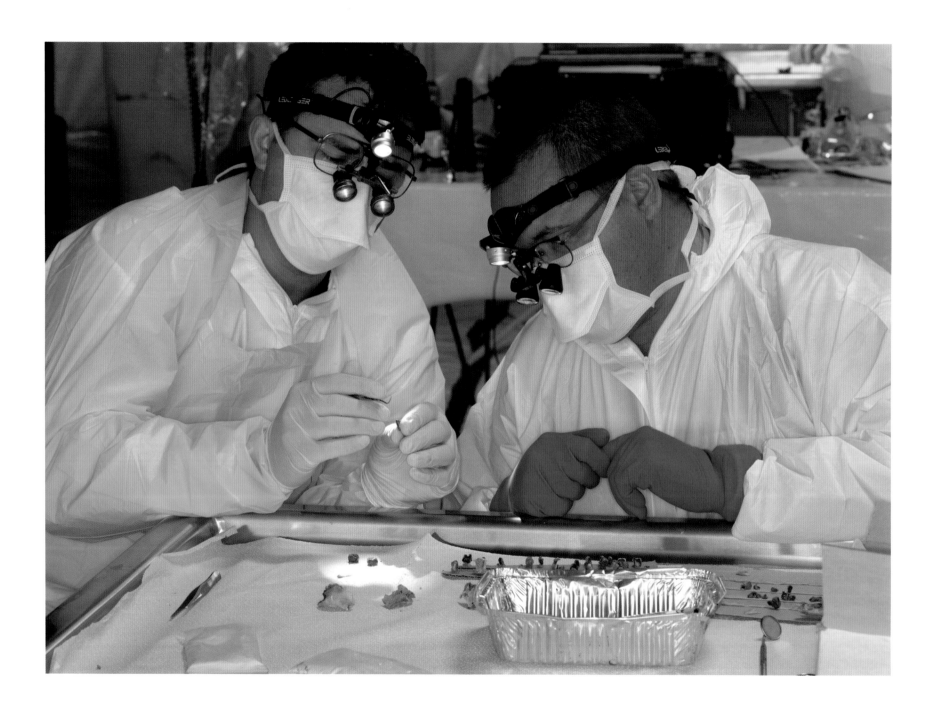

These pages and following: New Zealand police and a USAR team from the United States at Redcliffs. A massive landslide crushed houses in this seaside suburban street, causing the deaths of two people.

Above: Lyttelton — looking down Oxford Street towards the wharf.

Opposite: The Lava Bar, London Street, Lyttelton.

Above and opposite: Durham Street Methodist Church, the oldest stone church in Christchurch city. Three people died in the collapse of the building, while working to dismantle the church's pipe organ, damaged in the September 2010 earthquake.

Opposite and above left: Hotel Grand Chancellor.
Above right: looking west along Cashel Street.

Above: Latimer Square, the old Normal School.

Opposite: Police staff observe two minutes' silence on the banks of the Avon River at Cambridge Terrace, 12.51pm on Tuesday, 1 March, one week after the earthquake.

Staying

We don't know who, or where you are …
But if you think that you can get rid of us
by simply flicking the mat,
sweeping us away
with your yard broom,
you've got another think coming.

Every building which falls, boulder which rolls,
child who cries
in his or her sleep,
strengthens our resolve.

Be you a 'force of nature'
or malevolent spirit,
the legacy of broken roads, cracked pavements,
dust and mud pumping
from the veins

are as charms on a bracelet
where we are concerned.
With every shake, we add another
— a door, a window, a church steeple.
An empty home, a street full of people.
Those taken from us.

There will be no spring-cleaning here.
We will gather up these charms, recent memories
Wear them, jingling, jangling on our arms.
The din we make will exceed yours.
For you are not the custodian.

We still hold the key; it is ours!
The Devil himself has not the strength
To wrestle it from our grasp.

— Gary McCormick

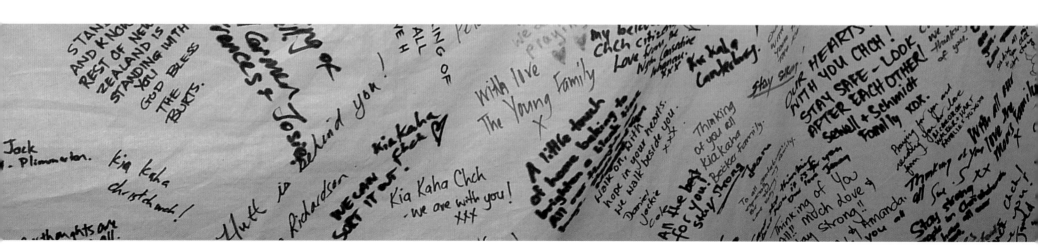